# street art

Adam Sutherland

Lerner Publications Company
**Minneapolis**

Street art should only be practiced in areas designated for legal street art or in a class situation under adult supervision.

First American edition published in 2012 by Lerner Publishing Group, Inc. Published by arrangement with Wayland, a division of Hachette Children's Books

Lerner Publications Company
A division of Lerner Publishing Group, Inc.
241 First Avenue North
Minneapolis, MN U.S.A.

Website address: www.lernerbooks.com

Library of Congress Cataloging-in-Publication Data

Sutherland, Adam.
    Street art / by Adam Sutherland. – 1st American ed.
       p.   cm. — (On the radar : street style)
    Includes index.
    ISBN 978–0–7613–7768–9 (lib. bdg. : alk. paper)
    1. Art and society—Juvenile literature.
    2.  Counterculture—Juvenile literature.  I. Title.
N72.S6S88  2012
709.05—dc23                         2011022304

Manufactured in the United States of America
  – CG – 12/15/11

Acknowledgments: Alamy: PixKicks 22–23; Flickr: Mathias Baert 15t, Ektopia 8l, Christy Gibney 1, 15b, Mrbaggins1 10l, Spleeny 14, Fredo Toulouse 12–13, www.mo-metalart.de 10t; Joshua Allen Harris: 2c, 16r, 16l, 17; Hedz: 2t, 21b; Rex: Mark Campbell 19; Shutterstock: Antoniomas 20–21, Thomas Barrat 4–5, 31b, Tomasz Bidermann 3l, 26, Philip Date 28–29, Songquan Deng 18, Emkaplin 30t, Vivian Fung 2b, 7t, 8b, Jitloac 3br, 6b, Willem van de Kerkhof 2–3, 29, Sabino Parente 30b, Andrej Pol 31t, Jeremy Reddington 24–25, Jose A.S. Reyes 28; Wikimedia: Jonathanryan 10r, Shrewdcat 1r; © Marlys Hansen/Independent Picture Service, 11l; Johannes Eisele/AFP/Getty Images 27.

Main body text set in
Helvetica Neue LT Std 13/15.5.
Typeface provided by Adobe Systems.

# cover stories

# CONTENTS

## thepeople

## theart

## thetalk

Street art is specially designed for the streets. It can be funny, surprising, and entertaining. It often makes people think more carefully about the streets they walk down. Street artists create sculptures, 3-D designs, and yarn art. They can even turn themselves into art, with mime artists, flash mobs, and living statues giving performances to passersby.

# STREET STYLE!

## Art for every environment!

Street artists use many different styles and locations to produce their work. For example, they might alter disused road signs to create something unique. They might use random, everyday objects (such as chewing gum stuck to a pavement!) to create colorful, eye-catching designs. That really is art on the street!

## Taking it to the streets

Some artists might make their art in a studio, then put it in a public place where they think it will have the most impact. Street-smart, quirky, and forever changing, street art can be anything the artist wants it to be. Go ahead and explore—the street is your canvas!

Artist Tony Tasset created EYE as a temporary art exhibit in Chicago in 2010.

## Turning junk into art!

Street artists can turn anything and everything into art. They can paint designs on cardboard boxes or make sculptures out of old plastic cups or garbage-can liners. The recycled nature of street art can help make the art cheap to create. Recycled street art also makes a point to governments about waste, and how people throw away too many things.

# ART IS THE WORD

Learn to speak the language of street art with On the Radar's handy guide!

**bronze**
a yellowish-brown mixture of copper and tin that is used to make sculptures

**cast**
a kind of hollow sculpture—in the shape of a human body, for example

**emulsion**
a type of paint with a matte effect

**fiberglass**
a light, strong material popular with street artists that is made from fine glass fibers

**flash mob**
a group of people who gather suddenly in a public place, perform an unusual piece of art, and then leave

**guerrilla art**
art created by a small organized group, sometimes politically motivated, working outside of the normal rules of society

**installation**
an artwork created when artists use 3-D objects and space

**living statue**
a mime artist who poses like a statue, sometimes for hours on end

**marble**
hard rock, often used for carving sculptures

**matte**
a non-shiny effect

**mural**
an image that is painted directly onto a wall

**tag**
a graffiti artist's basic style of signature, a little like their own logo

**3-D art**
three-dimensional letters and images

**yarn bombing**
covering street furniture, such as lampposts and railings, with yarn or crochet

Humor meets street sculpture as a workman surfaces from a manhole!

# GLOSSARY

**carve**
to cut or chip into a hard object to create a new shape

**class divide**
the separation between rich, often educated people and poor, often uneducated people

**commissioned**
to be asked to create a piece of art on behalf of another person or organization

**crochet**
to make something, usually out of wool or cotton, by looping and weaving thread with a hooked needle

**disposable**
designed to be thrown away

**disused**
thrown away, neglected, or not used

**endurance**
to do something for a long period of time

**illusion**
a false or misleading appearance; a deceptive view of reality

**influential**
someone or something in a position of importance

**innovative**
full of ideas; introducing new styles or new ways of doing something

**prime**
to apply a layer of special paint to prepare wood for painting

**subculture**
a small part of mainstream culture, with its own attitudes, beliefs, and influences

**tarot cards**
special cards with distinctive symbols used for telling people's fortunes

Street sculpture meets graffiti art! This cow street sculpture features a mural too.

A Mirko Flodin tire beast sculpture

One of the installations from Mark Jenkins's Embed series in Washington, D.C.

# CRAZY SCULPTURES

A fiberglass cow sculpture

Sculptures date back thousands of years and are traditionally carved from expensive, hard-to-find materials, such as marble or bronze. Street art sculptures are different. They are made of whatever the artist wants to use to create the biggest impact!

## The packing tape king

Mark Jenkins, a U.S. street artist, makes installations out of transparent packing tape. Mark has been known to cover parking meters with tape to make big lollipop heads and to take casts of his own body and leave them in surprising places around the city streets. His Embed series shows people's bodies disappearing into buildings!

## Galleries on the street

Imaginative street artists around the world are creating unusual sculptures such as the fiberglass cows that were part of a traveling exhibition called Cow Parade in 2006. It featured hundreds of eye-catching cow sculptures!

## On a mission

Since the 1970s, the Mission District in San Francisco, California, has been a rich and welcoming arena for street artists. The community embraces murals, stenciling, graffiti, and other art forms. The art showcases political and social messages, as well as humor and entertainment. Artists and businesses join together to celebrate the diversity and talent of the neighborhood.

## Tires turn into art

German sculptor Mirko Flodin turns recycled tires into great street art. His sculptures of horses, dragons, sharks, and other extraordinary beasts have been shown across Europe and Asia.

# GOING GLOBAL

From Melbourne, Australia, to Saint Paul, Minnesota, street artists are hard at work creating something new. Their work is bright, bold, and out in the open. Here are some of the highlights.

## Johannesburg, South Africa

Mary Sibande's series of street art images appeared around the city on billboards and on the sides of buildings in 2010. Mary creates fiberglass casts of her own body, which she paints black and dresses in colorful Victorian-style costumes. She then photographs the results to create striking, powerful images of lifelike dolls.

**Mary Sibande's dolls are dressed in elaborate costumes (left). People are often featured in Swoon's art (above).**

## New York, New York

Swoon is one of the world's most famous female street artists. She specializes in life-size prints and paper cutouts made of paste that are stuck to walls. Her work can also be seen in galleries such as the Museum of Modern Art.

Street art can be an ice sculpture *(below)* or a yarn-bombed tree *(right)*!

## London, England

Street artist, photographer, and blogger Slinkachu creates lifelike street scenes using miniature railway figures as models. His photographs show couples living on tennis-ball desert islands or rowing boats in puddles of spilled milk!

## Saint Paul, Minnesota

At the annual Winter Carnival, hardy artists take up their drills and hacksaws to create temporary ice sculptures out of blocks of ice. Working into the wee hours, the artists have 48 hours to complete their masterpieces.

## Melbourne, Australia

This south Australian city has one of the most active street art scenes in the world. Since 2004 it has hosted the annual 10-day Melbourne Stencil Festival. It has featured more than 800 works from 150 artists, as well as live demonstrations, artist talks, and workshops.

## Stockholm, Sweden

Members of the Swedish yarn-bombing collective Masquerade turn their environment into a colorful, knitted playground. They cover statues, trees, and lampposts. They even decorated the streets with knitted flowers! Their work can be seen throughout northern Europe.

# "TARZAN"

German street artist Johan Lorbeer created "Tarzan," an attention-grabbing performance piece that amazes audiences across Europe. Johan hangs above a crowd, seemingly stuck to the wall with his bare hand! But how does he do it?

## Essential technique

- Good head for heights
- Upper body strength
- Plenty of stamina
- Ability to stay still for long periods of time

## HOW IT'S DONE

1. The arm that is leaning against the wall is a fake arm.

2. The fake arm—strong enough to hold Johan's weight—is part of a metal frame. One end of the frame is attached to the wall, the rest is hidden inside Johan's clothes, running down his back, and attached to his shoes so that his weight is evenly distributed.

3. Johan is raised onto a building, and the fake arm and frame are attached to the wall. Because of the height, passersby cannot see the frame or the fact that the arm is not real!

## Why do it?

"Tarzan" is one of Johan's most famous performances. He hangs in the air for hours on end, barely moving or speaking. He looks almost like a statue, and the longer he goes without speaking, the more interested the crowd becomes. Johan has created a unique and memorable form of street art!

# GUERRILLA ART

Street art comes in all shapes and sizes! It's all about making an impact and spreading the message of art in the urban environment.

## Cardboard city

Adam Neate started painting on cardboard boxes left in the street because he could not afford canvases. He's become one of the most famous British street artists. Adam estimates he has left 5,000 works around London—and once left out 1,000 box designs in one night!

## Guerrilla gardening

Who says street art has to be limited to the concrete? Artists are using cities' green spaces too, planting vegetable patches in abandoned spots, or surprisingly colorful flower beds in pavement slabs that are missing. Guerrilla gardening brings color and life to urban environments across the United States and in parts of Europe.

## Knitting graffiti

A group of street artists from Texas, began the knit graffiti or yarn-bombing craze in 2005. Artists wrap lampposts, parking meters, and street signs with colorful knits and crochets to make street art a little more cozy! Groups have since sprung up worldwide, from New York and Sydney, Australia, to Mexico City.

Guerrilla gardening
in Ghent, Belgium

Crocheted by
yarn bombers!

# HOT-AIR ARTIST

## My story by Joshua Allen Harris

As a child, I loved drawing and painting but never thought I could do it for a living. After I left school, I spent 10 years working in retail but always regretted not pursuing art. So in 2005, I decided to go back to college to study.

When I was in college, I was fascinated by the street art I saw in New York. I decided that I also wanted to create something in the open for the public to see. One day, I saw a plastic shopping bag blowing in the wind, and it gave me an idea. At the time, there was a lot of talk of global warming and how the ice caps were melting. I decided to create a polar bear sculpture—using packing tape and shopping bags—and attached it to the subway grate. Whenever a train went by underground, the warm air would rise and bring the bear to life. When the train had passed, the bear deflated.

The polar bear really caught people's imaginations. One of the world's most influential art websites, the Wooster Collective, featured me on their home page. The next thing I knew I was doing interviews for CNN and other TV stations! My work has brought people together—it's been a wonderful experience.

# LEON REID IV

## Street art pioneer

### THE STATS

**Name:** Leon Reid IV
**Also known as:** VERBS, Darius Jones
**Born:** September 18, 1979
**Place of birth:** Richmond, Virginia
**Job:** Street artist

## Growing up with graffiti

Leon started out as a graffiti artist at the age of 15, using the street name VERBS. Leon's family had left his hometown of Richmond to move to Cincinnati, Ohio. Covering buildings with graffiti was all the rage, and Leon and his friends would leave their tags all over the city.

## The streets of New York

In 1998 the young artist moved to New York to study at the Pratt Institute, one of the most influential U.S. art schools. He dropped the name VERBS and began working as Darius Jones, progressing from spray-can art to 3-D street art. There, he met film students Quenell Jones and Brad Downey, and the three men became a street art trio. They disguised themselves as construction workers with hard hats and reflective vests. They traveled the city bending, welding, and reworking everyday objects, such as road signs and telephone boxes. Between them, they created around 150 amazing street art sculptures.

## Heading to London

The next stop was London, England, where Leon studied for a master's degree in fine art from 2003 to 2004. He kept producing his street sculptures. He enjoyed playing with road signs. One of his most famous pieces shows a silhouetted man catching his wife and child as they "fall off" a sign.

## Turning street art into money

Leon returned to the United States in 2005 and started working almost exclusively on projects that were commissioned by city councils, art festivals, and private companies. He is recognized around the world as a truly original and innovative street artist.

## Career highlights

**2003** Created *Fleur D'acier*, a steel rose that sprouted from the New York pavements!

**2008** Published *The Adventures of Darius and Downey*

**2009** Produced *True Yank*, a sculpture of President Lincoln for Urbis, a gallery in Manchester, England

Leon's *True Yank* sculpture shows President Abraham Lincoln wearing a Yankees baseball cap and hip-hop jewelry.

# MYLZ

Mylz, our On the Radar expert, is a street artist, DJ, and director of Hedz Ltd. This creative arts and design organization works with young people from all backgrounds. Here, he tells On the Radar what street art is and why it is his favorite art form.

## Did you enjoy art at school?

Actually, I found it pretty boring! I used to choose my own subjects to draw—cartoons or my favorite album covers—and then hand them in as coursework. They would get marked, so I guess my teacher could tell that I was inspired, even if it wasn't by his lessons!

## What is your definition of street art?

It is any artwork that reflects contemporary urban lifestyle and culture. Artists can choose to work in any form or with any materials that they feel reflect them best.

## How can you train to become a street artist?

Well, there are no street art training courses! My advice would be to figure out what types of street art you are interested in. Then find out who are the best artists producing these styles, and study their work. Follow that up with creating your own versions. Try not to copy other artists directly, but don't worry about taking influences—this is how many street artists develop their styles.

## How can I start creating street art?

If you want to be good, you need lots of practice, which you can't do in a hurry on the street. A cheap plank of wood can be a good starting point. Prime it with emulsion and then paint over it. Once you've done some artwork that you're happy with, mount it on your bedroom wall!

### What makes a great piece of street art?

A good idea and a clean, careful execution are all you need. The location can give a piece even more impact. If you create a work of art that totally transforms a boring or dull environment, it will really stand out!

### Where are the best places in the world to see street art?

New York and San Francisco are great. Bristol and Birmingham in Britain are very up-and-coming. Areas of London are really impressive. As street art gains more of a positive reputation, hopefully the artwork will gain respect and artistic areas within cities will be preserved.

# DAVID BLAINE

## THE STATS

**Name:** David Blaine
**Born:** April 4, 1973
**Place of birth:** Brooklyn, New York
**Nationality:** American
**Job:** Street artist, magician, endurance artist

## The young illusionist

David Blaine became fascinated with cards and illusions by watching his grandmother give tarot card readings. He picked up a deck of playing cards when he was five years old and says he has been practicing ever since. At a young age, David also developed an early taste for risking life and limb. He still has a scar on the bridge of his nose where an attempted backflip off a park bench went wrong!

## Suffering for art

More recently, David has moved toward his own form of installation street art. He blends illusion and performance with a series of endurance feats, watched by audiences around the world. His "Frozen in Time" stunt in 2000 required him to be encased in a block of ice for nearly 64 hours in the middle of New York's Times Square. For "Vertigo" in 2002, David stood on top of a 100-foot (30-meter) pillar for 35 hours! For his "Drowned Alive" feat in New York in 2006 *(pictured here)*, David immersed himself in a giant sphere of water for one week.

## Magic man

After leaving home at 17, David supported himself in New York by performing magic tricks at private parties. He then moved to southern France, where he performed at the mansions of millionaires. These days, David can still make around $100,000 per night for a private show! In 1997 his first TV special *David Blaine: Street Magic* was broadcast. The young performer focused more on the audience's reaction to his tricks and adapted them in response. This added an exciting new element to a traditional form of entertainment.

## What's next?

David is a master of holding his breath. He broke the world record live on TV in 2008 when he held his breath for 17 minutes and 4.4 seconds on *The Oprah Winfrey Show.* David is always searching for the next great showstopping street art performance. With his constant drive to entertain and his willingness to try never-before-seen acts of skill and endurance, David is one of the most exciting street performers in the world!

# STREET STATS!

## 1:87

## 3

The number of hours street artist Joshua Allen Harris needed to create his *Subway Sea Monster* sculpture from plastic bags.

The scale of the model people in artist Slinkachu's work. In other words, they are $1/87$th of their real size.

# WHAT ARE YOU LOOKING AT?

## 2004

The year that the term *flash mob* was added to the dictionary.

## $1.57
### MILLION

The estimated value of artworks distributed in one night by Adam Neate on November 14, 2008.

# 1,000

Estimated number of legal street artworks on view in Melbourne, Australia.

# 40

The number of cities around the world taking part in the flash-mob event, International Pillow Fight Day 2011.

# 3,822

The number of minutes David Blaine was encased in ice in New York's Time Square for his stunt "Frozen in Time."

# 1973

The year guerrilla gardening began in New York.

Zombies flash mobbed
Warsaw, Poland, in 2009.

# THE FLASH MOB

In the age of instant communication via the Internet and mobile phones, a unique form of street performance has emerged. This street style is called the flash mob, and it's coming to a town near you!

## The birth of the flash mob

Journalist Bill Wasik claims to have created the flash mob movement in 2003. Coordinating four groups in separate New York hot spots, he arranged for more than 100 people to meet in the rug department of Macy's. The crowd all claimed to be roommates who were shopping for a new rug and always made their buying decisions together! Bill's next performances were a 15-second spontaneous round of applause in a hotel lobby and an invasion of a shoe shop by a group claiming to be foreign tourists!

## The art of dancing

In 2009, to celebrate the end of Oprah Winfrey's 25 years of hosting *The Oprah Winfrey Show*, her staff arranged a huge flash mob. More than 20,000 people surprised the legendary interviewer. Black Eyed Peas performed their hit "I Gotta Feeling" live, while fans danced to choreographed moves in groups that stretched for blocks in downtown Chicago. It was the world's largest flash mob in a single spot!

## Fighting with feathers

One of the most successful and long-running flash mobs is International Pillow Fight Day. The first event took place in March 2008, with more than 25 cities around the world participating. In New York, more than 5,000 people attended. The 2011 event took place in cities from Toronto, Canada, to Istanbul, Turkey. Organizer Kevin Bracken thinks the phenomenon is showing no signs of stopping.

These people throw pillows at one another in Berlin, Germany, during the annual International Pillow Fight Day in 2011.

# STILL AS A STATUE

You are frozen perfectly still, eyes closed. The only time you open them is when someone drops a coin into the container at your feet. Your arms are set into position on your lap. Your shoulders droop as you slump slightly on the uncomfortable wooden stool. But you have to stay in character—the statue, unmoving, as still as stone.

## Get prepared!

You have worked on your outfit for weeks, painting and shading the dress, accessories, and shoes to look just right. It's your finished masterpiece. You decided to paint your face and hands this morning on the street—you didn't want to get on the train in the full costume! Your face paint is as thick as mud, itchy, and uncomfortable. You are pleased it's not a hot day—that would be unbearable!

## Time for action

A small, curious crowd has gathered—a few tourists and some mothers with small children. It's amazing what you can sense, even with your eyes closed! You cannot make the smallest movement. The children's eyes are as big as saucers as they watch you. Then a little girl drops a coin into your pot. Slowly, you come to life. You must climb off your chair and bow in thanks to her. There are laughs and a little applause from the crowd as you slowly climb back onto your stool.

## Feeling the strain

The day has been a success, but your shoulders ache from holding your arms in one place and from the effort of keeping them so still. As the final shopper leaves the street, you leave your seat. Your joints creak like old doors, glad of the movement. You look forward to the journey home. The life of a statue is harder than people think!

# ART FOR ALL?

FOR

Fans love street art for its free expression and the way it brings city streets to life. They say:

1. Street art allows everyone to express themselves, whether rich or poor. People can start by painting on cardboard boxes or scraps of wood if they cannot afford other materials.
2. Street artists make people look at and appreciate the urban environment in a whole new way.
3. Artists such as Leon Reid IV and Slinkachu have put street art on the map. They have attracted a lot of new fans who want to be part of a cool, mysterious, underground subculture.
4. Environmentally friendly and using all kinds of disused materials, street art is the ultimate in recycling!
5. There is no class divide and no snobbery with street art. It is not hidden away in art galleries. It is out in the open for everyone to see and enjoy.
6. Street artists are in touch with their audience and have a better idea of what interests them than traditional artists.
7. A regular feature in art galleries, street art can be regarded as just as important and well-respected as traditional art.

However, some people think that street art is antisocial and is spoiling our environment. They say:

1. Street art created without the permission of a city council or a property owner is illegal and no better than vandalism.
2. Thousands of dollars worth of damage to buildings and street signs can be caused by street artists who do not respect public property.
3. Artists trying to create new, unexpected pieces of street art might take unnecessary risks and injure themselves.
4. Crowds gathering to look at street art or to take part in flash mobs can cause obstructions in busy pedestrian areas, shops, and hotels.

# AGAINST

## Right or wrong?

Street art can bring city streets to life and is a great way for people to express themselves. Making sculptures out of packing tape or creating disposable artwork on cardboard is imaginative and harms no one. As long as street artists respect other people's property and do not damage it, street art can be enjoyed and supported by everyone.

# GET MORE INFO

## Books

Gogerly, Liz. *Graffiti Culture*. Minneapolis: Lerner Publications Company, 2012. This book gives an overview of how graffiti—another type of street art—has changed the urban scene.

Gogerly, Liz. *Street Dance*. Minneapolis: Lerner Publications Company, 2012. This title shows the fusion between dance and street art.

Marceau, Marcel, and Bruce Goldstone. *Bip in a Book*. New York: Harry N. Abrams, 2001. Photographs tell the story of Bip, the alter-ego of the famous French mime Marcel Marceau and Bip's efforts to escape being trapped in a book.

Raczka, Bob. *3-D ABC: A Sculptural Alphabet*. Minneapolis: Millbrook Press, 2007. This colorful book shows a variety of museum and urban sculptures.

Walters, Eric. *In a Flash*. Victoria, BC: Orca Book Publishers, 2008. In this novel, Ian and his two closest friends organize flash mobs for fun or to push for change.

## Websites

**David Blaine's Official Website**
**http://davidblaine.com/**
Learn more about this daring street artist at his official website.

**International Street Art**
**http://unurth.com/**
This site brings together images of amazing street art from around the world—and not just in urban areas.

**Streetsy**
**http://www.streetsy.com/about**
Taking its cue from the famous graffiti artist Banksy, this website celebrates the latest street art shared by fans of this urban art form.

**The Wooster Collective**
**http://www.woostercollective.com/**
Founded in New York in 2001, this group dedicates its website to showcasing street art found in cities around the world.

# INDEX